M000206323

PREPARING FOR THE DAY OF JUDGEMENT

PREPARING FOR THE DAY OF JUDGEMENT

by

Imām Ibn Ḥajar al-ʿAsqalānī

TRANSLATED BY

S. M. HASAN AL-BANNA

AWAKENING

PUBLISHED BY THE PRESS SYNDICATE OF AWAKENING PUBLICATIONS
Uplands Business Centre, Bernard Street, Swansea, SA2 0DR, United Kingdom

AWAKENING PUBLICATIONS
Uplands Business Centre, Bernard Street, Swansea, SA2 0DR, United Kingdom
P.O. Box 360009, Milpitas, CA 95036, United States of America
© Awakening Publications 2004

This book is in copyright. Subject to statutory exception and to the provisions of relevant collective licensing agreements, no reproduction of any part may take place without the written permission of Awakening Publications.

First Published in August 2004/Jumada al-Thani 1425

Typeset in Bembo 11/14 [CP]

A catalogue record for this book is available from the British Library
Library of Congress cataloging in publication data
Preparing for the Day of Judgement
Imām Ibn Ḥājar al-ʿAsqalānī p. cm.
Includes bibliographical references
ISBN 0 9543294 3 0 1. Islam - Spirituality. 1.Title.
BP66.G7M38 2004
297.049109032- 97-41875 CIP

Special thanks to Bara, Yusra, Intissar and Suhaib

بسم الله الرحمن الرحيم

Abū'l-Faḍl Shihāb al-Dīn Aḥmad ibn ʿAlī al-Kannānī al ʿAsqalānī, better known by the name of Imām Ibn Ḥajar, was born in Cairo in 773/1372. He began his studies at the age of five and completed the memorisation of the Qur'an by the age of nine. A Shāfiʿī scholar and hadith master, he studied under renowned scholars in Cairo, Yemen, and the Ḥijāz. Known as Shaykh al-Islām, scholars travelled from far away lands to take knowledge from him. Appointed to the position of chief-judge several times, he authored more than fifty works on hadith, history, biography, Qur'anic exegesis, poetry, and Shāfiʿī jurisprudence; among the most famous of them is his fourteen-volume commentary on Ṣaḥīḥ al-Bukhārī called Fatḥ al-Bārī. He passed away in Cairo in 852/1449.

CONTENT

FOREWORD

Praise be to Allah Lord of the universe, Creator and Sustainer of mankind; and may His peace and blessings be upon our beloved Messenger Muḥammad ﷺ, his family, Companions, and those who follow them until the Day of Judgement.

When Allah the Almighty, in His infinite wisdom and divine mercy, created the human soul, He intended its eternal abode to be in the Garden of Bliss. However, the journey to this eternal abode is indeed full of many obstacles, be it the splendours of this world, the passions of our lower self (*nafs*), or the whispers of Satan. It is the successful preparation for this journey that will – with the Mercy of Allah – ultimately lead us to that Garden. This preparation is based on comprehending the Divine Message and internalising its teachings in our lives. Many a noble and strong-willed soul has undertaken this journey, and what lies in these pages are the valuable pieces of advice that represent the fruits of their experience.

A Prophetic tradition states, "Wisdom is the lost property of the believer. If he finds it then he is most deserving of it." This book is a beautiful compilation of some of the wise sayings of the Prophet ﷺ, of the Companions, and of the pious predecessors and ascetics. Reflecting on these wise sayings and heeding these counsels will assist in infusing us with the requisite awareness and fervour to prepare for the Day of Judgement. Verily, we are in need of such counsel, for our Day of Judgement begins not when the world ends, but when our life comes to an end – which is indeed imminent – as the Prophet ﷺ stated.

The author, Imām Ibn Ḥājar al-ʿAsqalānī – a scholar of immense stature, especially in the field of hadith – adopted a unique approach in compiling these sayings. He ordered these sayings numerically, beginning each chapter with Prophetic traditions followed by sayings of the Companions, then those of the pious predecessors. This arrangement bears testimony to his encyclopedic knowledge and creativity.

May the immense wisdom contained in this book enlighten our hearts, open our eyes and awaken us from our state of heedlessness to our real task in this *dunyā* – preparing for the Day of Judgement, as Allah the Almighty says, *For surely it is not the eyes that are blind, but it is the hearts that are in the chests.*

S. M. Hasan al-Banna
July 2004
London, UK

I

Counsel in Twos

[1]
It has been narrated that the Prophet ﷺ said, "There are two traits, nothing is better than them: belief in Allah and bringing benefit to the Muslims. And there are two traits, nothing is worse than them: associating partners with Allah and bringing harm to the Muslims."

[2]
The Prophet ﷺ said, "Sit with the scholars and listen to the speech of the wise, for verily Allah the Exalted gives life to the dead heart with the light of wisdom as he gives life to the dead soil with rainwater."

[3]
Abū Bakr al-Ṣiddīq ؓ said, "He who enters the grave without any provisions is as though he wishes to sail the sea without a ship."

[4]
ʿUmar ibn al-Khaṭṭāb ؓ said, "Honour in this world is in wealth, and honour in the Hereafter is in righteous actions."

[5]

ʿUthmān ibn ʿAffān said, "Worrying about the *dunyā* is a darkness in the heart, while worrying about the Hereafter is a light in the heart."

[6]

ʿAlī ibn Abī Ṭālib said, "The one who seeks after knowledge, Paradise will seek after him; and the one who seeks after disobedience, the Hellfire will seek after him."

[7]

Yaḥyā ibn Muʿādh said, "An honourable person would never be disobedient to Allah, and a wise person would never prefer the *dunyā* over the Hereafter."

[8]

Al-Aʿmash said, "The one whose capital is God-consciousness (*taqwā*), tongues will be incapable of describing the fortune that is his piety; and the one whose capital is the *dunyā*, tongues will be incapable of describing the magnitude of his loss of piety."

[9]

Sufyān al-Thawrī said, "Every act of disobedience committed due to passion, its forgiveness is hoped for. Every act of disobedience committed due to arrogance, its forgiveness is not hoped for because the root of Satan's disobedience was arrogance, whereas the root of Adam's lapse was passion."

[10]

An ascetic once said, "The one who sins while laughing, Allah will make him enter the Fire while crying. And the one who obeys while crying (out of fear of Allah), Allah will make him enter Paradise while laughing."

[11]

A wise man said, "Do not belittle minor sins, for verily from them major sins grow."

[12]
The Prophet ﷺ said, "No sin remains minor when accompanied by persistence, and no sin remains major when accompanied by the seeking of forgiveness."

[13]
It is said, "The Gnostic (*ʿārif*) occupies himself with praise [of Allah], while the ascetic (*zāhid*) occupies himself with supplication; because the Gnostic's concern is his Lord, while the ascetic's concern is his own nafs."

[14]
A sage said, "Whoever is under the delusion that he has a closer friend than Allah, little is his knowledge of Allah; and the one who is under the delusion that he has a greater enemy than his nafs, little is his knowledge of his nafs."

[15]
Abū Bakr al-Ṣiddīq ﷺ said regarding the Qur'anic verse, 'Corruption has appeared on land and sea', "The land refers to the tongue and the sea refers to the heart. If the tongue is corrupted people cry over it, and if the heart is corrupted the angels cry over it.

[16]
It is said, "Verily passion turns kings into slaves, and patience turns slaves into kings... Do you not see the story of Yūsuf and Zulaykha?"

[17]
It is said, "Glad tidings to the one whose intellect is his master and whose desire is his slave. And woe to the one whose desire is his master and whose intellect is his slave."

[18]
It is also said, "The one who leaves sins, his heart will be softened; and the one who leaves the forbidden and eats the lawful, his intellect will be enlightened."

[19]
Allah revealed to one of the Prophets, "Obey me in that which I have commanded you, and do not disobey me in that which I have advised you."

[20]
It is said, "The perfection of the intellect is in following the pleasure of Allah and avoiding His wrath."

[21]
It is said, "There is no exile for the learned, and there is no homeland for the ignorant."

[22]
It is said, "The one who is close to Allah due to his obedience will be a stranger amongst people."

[23]
It is said, "The movement towards obedience is evidence of knowledge just as the movement of the body is evidence of its vitality."

[24]
The Prophet ﷺ said, "The root of all sins is love of the *dunyā* and the root of all tribulations is withholding taxes and *zakāt*."

[25]
It is said, "The one who admits his shortcomings is always praised, and admitting shortcomings is a sign of acceptance [by Allah]."

[26]
It is said, "Ingratitude for blessings is baseness and the company of a fool is bad fortune."

[27]
A poet said:

O he who is busy with his *dunyā*!
Whom illusions of a long lifetime have deluded
Was he not in a state of heedlessness
Until his appointed time drew near?

Verily death arrives suddenly
And the Grave is the collection-box of actions
Be patient over the *dunyā* and its hardships
No death is there except at one's appointed time

2

\\ \/

Counsel in Threes

[1]

It has been reported that the Prophet ﷺ said, "The one who wakes up in the morning and complains about the scarcity of livelihood, it is as though he is complaining against his Lord. The one who wakes up and is sad over the affairs of the *dunyā*, it is as though he has woken up angry with Allah. And the one who humbles himself in front of a rich man because of his wealth will have lost two-thirds of his Religion."

[2]

Abū Bakr al-Ṣiddīq ؓ said, "There are three things which cannot be attained through another three: wealth with hope, youth with dyeing [the hair], and health with medication."

[3]

ʿUmar ibn al-Khaṭṭāb ؓ said, "Good interaction with people is half of intelligence, good questioning is half of knowledge, and good planning is half of subsistence."

[4]

ʿUthmān ibn ʿAffān ﷺ said, "The one who leaves the *dunyā* Allah the Exalted will love him; and the one who leaves sins, the Angels will love him; and the one who has no craving for the possessions of the Muslims, the Muslims will love him."

[5]

ʿAlī ibn Abī Ṭālib ﷺ said, "Surely from the blessings of this world, sufficient is Islam as a blessing; surely from the multitude of preoccupations, sufficient is obedience as a preoccupation; and surely from the causes for reflection, sufficient is death as a cause."

[6]

ʿAbdullāh ibn Masʿūd ﷺ said, "How many are deluded by the blessings showered on them; how many are tested by the praise heaped on them; and how many are duped into a sense of security by Allah hiding their sins."

[7]

Prophet Dāwūd said, "It was revealed to me in the Psalms that a sensible person should only occupy himself with three things - making provisions for the Day of Judgement, seeking sustenance for his life, and seeking pleasure within what is permissible."

[8]

Abū Hurayra ﷺ related that the Prophet ﷺ said, "There are three saviours and three damnations, three [high] ranks and three absolutions. As for the saviours, they are: fearing Allah the Exalted in secret and in public, spending moderately in poverty and in richness, and justice in contentment and in anger. As for the damnations, they are: severe miserliness, following one's desires, and self-infatuation. As for the [high] ranks, they are: spreading the greeting of *salām*, providing food (for guests, as well as the poor and needy), and praying at night whilst people are asleep. As for the absolutions, they are: making ablution in cold nights, walking to the congregational prayers, and awaiting the next prescribed prayer having just finished a prescribed prayer [in the mosque]."

[9]

Jibrā'īl said, "O Muḥammad! Live as long as you will, for you will surely die; love whomsoever you wish, for you will leave them; and do whatever you wish, for you will be recompensed accordingly."

[10]

The Prophet ﷺ said, "There are three individuals whom Allah will shade under the shade of His Throne on a day when there will be no shade except His shade - the one who makes ablution in difficult conditions, the one who walks to the mosque in the darkness, and the one who feeds the hungry."

[11]

It was said to Prophet Ibrāhīm عليه السلام, "Why did Allah take you as a friend?" He said, "For three things - I always chose Allah's commands over the commands of others; I never worried about what Allah had already allotted for me (of livelihood); and I never lunched and supped except with a guest."

[12]

A wise man said, "Three things drive away anguish - remembrance of Allah, meeting His *awliyā'* (those close to Him), and talking to sages."

[13]

Al-Ḥasan al-Baṣrī said, "He who has no manners has no knowledge; he who has no patience has no Religion (*dīn*); and he who has no God-consciousness has no closeness to Allah."

[14]

It has been narrated that a man from Banī Isrā'īl went to seek knowledge and their prophet came to hear of this. He called for the man and said to him, "O young man! I will tell you of three things in which lies the knowledge of all those who have come and all those to come - fear Allah in secret and public, hold your tongue regarding people and do not speak of them except in goodness, and ensure that the bread that you eat is *ḥalāl*." Upon hearing this, the young man refrained from leaving [to seek knowledge].

[15]

It has been narrated that a man from Banī Isrā'īl collected eighty chests full of scriptures and books of knowledge but did not benefit from his knowledge. Allah the Exalted revealed to their prophet to say to this collector, "Even if you had collected a lot of knowledge it will not benefit you except if you do three things - do not love the *dunyā* for it is not a home for the believers; do not befriend Satan for he is not a companion for the believers; and do not hurt anyone for that is not the way of the believers."

[16]

It is reported that Abū Sulaymān al-Dārānī said in his supplication, "O my Lord, if you ask me about my many sins, I will surely ask You for Your forgiveness; and if you ask me about my miserliness, I will surely ask You for Your generosity; and if you make me enter Hell, I will inform the people of Hell that I love You."

[17]

It is said, "The happiest of all people is he who has a sincere heart, a patient body, and contentment with what he possesses."

[18]

Ibrāhīm al-Nakhaʿī said, "Those who were destroyed before you were destroyed due to three traits - excess in speech, excess in food, and excess in sleep."

[19]

Yaḥyā ibn Muʿādh al-Rāzī said, "Glad tidings to the one who leaves the *dunyā* before it leaves him, prepares for his grave before he enters it, and pleases his Lord before he meets Him."

[20]

ʿAlī ibn Abī Ṭālib ﵁ said, "He who does not have the *sunnah* of

Allah, the *sunnah* of His Messenger, and the *sunnah* of His chosen ones, has nothing. It was asked, "What is the *sunnah* of Allah?" He replied, "Safeguarding secrets." It was asked, "What is the *sunnah* of the Messenger?" He replied, "Being gentle with people." It was asked, "What is the *sunnah* of His chosen ones?" He replied, "Bearing people's harm."

[21]

ʿAlī رضي الله عنه also said, "People before us used to advise each other of three things - the one who works for his Hereafter, Allah will take care of the matters of his *dīn* and *dunyā* for him; and the one who beautifies his inner self, Allah will beautify his appearance; and the one who rectifies that which is between him and Allah, Allah will rectify that which is between him and people."

[22]

ʿAlī رضي الله عنه also said: 'Be in Allah's estimation the best of people, and in the estimation of your nafs the worst of people, and in people's estimation just a man from amongst the people.'

[23]

It was said that Allah revealed to Prophet ʿUzayr, "O ʿUzayr! If you committed a small sin, do not look at its smallness; rather look at Whom you have sinned against. If you are granted a small blessing, do not look at its smallness; rather look at the One who has granted it to you. And if a calamity befalls you, then do not complain against Me to My creation, just as I do not complain against you to My angels when your bad deeds are raised to Me."

[24]

Ḥātim al-Aṣamm said, "There is not a morning that passes except that Satan says to me, 'What do you eat? What do you wear? Where do you live?' I say to him, 'I eat death, I wear the shroud, and I live in the grave.'"

[25]

The Prophet ﷺ said, "The one who comes out of the humiliation of disobedience into the honour of obedience, Allah the Exalted will make him rich without wealth, strengthen him without soldiers, and honour him without a clan."

[26]

It has been reported that he ﷺ went out to his companions and said, "How do you find yourselves this morning?" They replied, "As believers in Allah." He said, "What is the sign of your *īmān* (belief)?" They replied, "We are patient in times of hardship, grateful in times of ease, and content with whatever has been predestined." The Prophet ﷺ said, "By the Lord of the Kaʿba, you are truly believers!"

[27]

Allah revealed to one of the Prophets, "Whoever meets Me [on the Day of Judgement] while he loves Me, I will make him enter My Paradise. Whoever meets Me while he fears Me, I will spare him My Hell. And whoever meets Me and is ashamed because of his sins, I will make the angels who record deeds forget his sins."

[28]

ʿAbdullāh ibn Masʿūd said, "Fulfil that which Allah has made obligatory upon you and you will be the best of worshippers; refrain from the prohibitions of Allah and you will be the best of ascetics; and be pleased with what Allah has allotted for you and you will be the richest of people."

[29]

Ṣāliḥ al-Marqadiyy once passed by some houses and said, "Where are your first inhabitants? And where are your old dwellers?" So he heard a voice saying, "Their legacy has come to an end, underneath the soil their bodies have decomposed, and their actions remain as necklaces around their necks."

[30]

ʿAlī 🕮 said, "Give to whomsoever you wish and you will become his master; ask from whomever you wish and you will become his prisoner; and do not seek help from whomsoever you wish and you will be his equal."

[31]

Yaḥyā ibn Muʿādh said, "Leaving all of the *dunyā* is taking all of the *dunyā*: the one who leaves all of it has taken all of it and the one who takes all of it has left all of it; so, taking it is leaving it, and leaving it is taking it."

[32]

It was said to Ibrāhīm ibn al-Adham, "How did you attain *zuhd* (asceticism)?" "With three things," He said, "I saw that the grave is lonesome and that I would have no companion therein; I saw that the path is long while I had no provisions; and I saw that the Omnipotent would be the Judge while I had no valid argument (in my defence)."

[33]

Shiblī said, "O my Lord! I wish to gift to you all of my good deeds despite my poverty [in acts of obedience] and weakness; how then do You not wish, O my Master, to gift to me [the overlooking of] my bad deeds despite Your richness?!" He also said, "If you find delight in Allah's company then renounce the company of your nafs." And he said, "Had you tasted the sweetness of closeness to Allah you would have known the bitterness of estrangement (from Him)."

[34]

Sufyān al-Thawrī was asked about the sweetness of closeness to Allah the Exalted. He replied, "It is that you do not find delight in a beautiful face, nice voice, or eloquent tongue."

[35]

Ibn ʿAbbās 🕮 said, '*Zuhd* (asceticism) is composed of three letters, z-h-d. 'Z' is *zādun lil maʿād* [provision for the Hereafter]. 'H' is *hudan lil-dīn* [guidance for the Religion]. And 'D' is *dawām ʿalā al-ṭāʿa* [constancy in obedience]."

[36]

Ibn ʿAbbās ﵁ also said, "*Zuhd* (asceticism) is composed of three letters, z-h-d. 'Z' is for leaving *zīna* [adornments], 'H' is for leaving *hawā* [desires], and 'D' is leaving the *dunyā* [this world]."

[37]

A man once came to Ḥāmid al-Laffāf and said to him, "Advise me." He said, "Have for your Religion (*dīn*) a cover, just like a copy of the Qur'an (*muṣḥaf*) has a cover." The man asked, "And what is the cover of the *dīn*?" He replied, "Leaving speech except that which is necessary, leaving the *dunyā* except that which is necessary, and refraining from mixing with people except when it is necessary. Also know that the essence of asceticism is refraining from the prohibitions be they minor or major, fulfilling all the obligations be they easy or difficult, and leaving the things of this world for its people be they great or small."

[38]

Luqmān al-Ḥakīm, peace be upon him, said to his son, "O my son! Man is composed of three thirds - a third for Allah, a third for himself and a third for the worms. The third that is for Allah is his soul; the third that is for himself is his actions, and the third that is for the worms is his body."

[39]

ʿAlī ﵁ said, "Three things enhance memorisation and eradicate phlegm - *siwāk*, fasting, and reading the Qur'an."

[40]

Kaʿb al-Aḥbār ﵁ said, "Fortresses for the believers are three - the mosque is a fortress, the remembrance of Allah is a fortress, and reading the Qur'an is a fortress."

[41]

A wise man said, "Three things are from the treasures of Allah the Exalted that He does not give except to those He loves - poverty, illness, and patience."

[42]

Ibn ʿAbbās was once asked, "Which is the best of days? Which is the best of months? Which is the best of actions?" He replied, "The best of days is Friday, the best of months is Ramadan, and the best of actions is performing the five daily prayers in their prescribed times." After three days ʿAlī came to hear of the questions and the answers of Ibn ʿAbbās. ʿAlī said, "If the scholars, the sages, and the jurists of the East and the West were asked, they would not have replied as well as Ibn ʿAbbās, except that I say, "The best of actions is that which Allah accepts from you, the best of months is the month in which you make sincere repentance to Allah, and the best of days is the day in which you leave the world to [meet] Allah the Exalted while you are a believer."

[43]

A poet said:

> Do you not see how the two ever-renewables [night and day]
> Wear us out, while we jest in secret and in public?
> Trust not this world and its pleasures
> For its homes are not real homes
> And work for your benefit before your death
> And be not deceived by the abundance of friends and brothers

[44]

It is said that, "If Allah wants good for His servant He gives him the understanding of the *dīn*, reduces his attachment to the *dunyā*, and grants him awareness of his faults."

[45]

The Messenger of Allah ﷺ said, "I was made to love three things from your world - perfume, women, and prayer." The companions were sitting with him and Abū Bakr said, "You have spoken the truth, O Messenger of Allah! I was made to love three things from this world – looking at the face of the Messenger of Allah ﷺ, spending my wealth for the Messenger of Allah ﷺ, and giving my daughter in marriage to the Messenger of Allah ﷺ." ʿUmar ؓ said, "You have spoken truthfully, O Abū Bakr! I was made to love three things from this world – commanding good, forbidding evil, and worn garments." ʿUthmān ؓ said, "You have spoken truthfully, O ʿUmar! And I was made to love three things from this world – feeding the hungry, clothing the naked, and reading the Qur'an." ʿAlī ؓ said, "You have spoken truthfully, O ʿUthmān! I was made to love three things from this world – serving the guest, fasting in the summer, and fighting with the sword." As they were discoursing, Jibrā'īl came and said, "Allah the Exalted sent me when He heard your discussion and has ordered you to ask me what I would have loved if I were to be from the people of this world. The Messenger of Allah ﷺ asked, "If you were to be from the people of this world what would you have loved?" Jibrā'īl replied, "Guiding those led astray, keeping the company of contented strangers, and helping families afflicted with hardship." He continued, "The Lord of Honour loves three things from His servants – giving one's utmost, crying when in regret, and being patient in times of poverty."

[46]
A sage said, "The one who only considers his own opinion as correct will be misguided; the one who thinks he is rich due to his wealth will be impoverished; and the one who seeks prominence through a creature will be humiliated."

[47]
A sage said, "The fruits of *maʿrifa* (gnosis, intimate knowledge of Allah) are three – being ashamed from Allah the Exalted, loving Him, and enjoying His company."

[48]
The Prophet ﷺ said, "Love is the basis of *maʿrifa*, chastity is the sign

of conviction, and the peak of conviction is God-consciousness and contentment with what Allah the Exalted has predestined."

[49]
Sufyān ibn ʿUyaynah said, "Whoever loves Allah, Allah will make him love those whom He loves; and the one who loves those whom Allah the Exalted loves, Allah will make him love that which has made Him love them; and the one who loves that which made Allah the Exalted love those whom He loves will wish that no one knew him."

[50]
The Prophet ﷺ said, '"Truthfulness of love is in three things - choosing the speech of the beloved over the speech of others, choosing the company of the beloved over the company of others, and choosing the pleasure of the beloved over the pleasure of others."

[51]
Wahb ibn Munabbih al-Yamānī said, "It is written in the Torah that he who is greedy is in fact poor even if he owns the whole world; he who obeys [God] is obeyed even if he is a slave; and he who is content is rich even if he is hungry."

[52]
A wise man said, "The one who knows Allah will not find any pleasure in the company of creatures; the one who knows the world will not desire anything from it; and the one who knows the justice of Allah the Exalted will not feel the need to present his grievances to Him in order to obtain redress."

[53]
Dhū al-Nūn al-Miṣrī said, "Anyone who really fears something flees from it; anyone who really desires something seeks it; and anyone who finds the [sweetness of the] company of Allah becomes estranged from his nafs."

[54]

Dhū al-Nūn al-Miṣrī also said, "The one who knows Allah the Exalted is a captive, his heart is seeing, and his actions for Allah are many."

[55]

He also said, "The one who knows Allah the Exalted is loyal, his heart is alert, and his actions for Allah are pure."

[56]

Ibn Sulaymān al-Dārānī said, "The origin of every good in this world and the Hereafter is fear of Allah; the key to the *dunyā* is satiety; and the key to the Hereafter is hunger."

[57]

It is said that worship is a craft: its marketplace is isolation, its capital is God-consciousness, and its profit is Paradise.

[58]

Mālik ibn Dīnār said, "Remedy three things with three - pride with humility, greed with contentment, and envy with sincere advice."

3

Counsel in Fours

[1]

The Messenger of Allah ﷺ said to Abū Dharr al-Ghifārī, "O Abū Dharr! Mend the ship for the sea is deep, take all of the provisions for the journey is long, lighten the load for the obstacles are difficult, and make sincere your actions for the Critic is All-Seeing."

[2]

A poet said:

It is an obligation upon people to repent.
But leaving sins is even more of an obligation.
Patience in the midst of hardships is difficult to bear.
But losing the opportunity for reward is more difficult to bear.
Time is indeed perplexing in the way it passes.
Yet people's heedlessness is even more perplexing.
Everything that is due to arrive is indeed close,
Yet death is closer than everything else.

[3]

A sage said, "Four things are good but four others are even better - chastity is good in men, but in women it is even better; justice is good in lay people, but in rulers it is even better; repentance by an old man is good, but by a young man it is even better; and contentment by the rich is good, but by the poor it is even better."

[4]

A wise man said, "Four things are bad but four others are even worse - sinning is bad from a young man, but from an old man it is even worse; busying oneself with the *dunyā* is bad from an ignorant person, but from a scholar it is even worse; laziness in fulfilling religious obligations is bad from laymen, but from scholars and students of knowledge it is even worse; and pride is bad from the rich, but from the poor it is even worse."

[5]

Abū Bakr al-Ṣiddīq ﷺ said, "Four things are completed by four others - prayer with the Two Prostrations of Forgetfulness (*sajdatay al-sahw*), fasting [Ramadan] with *ṣadaqat al-fiṭr* (alms given at the end of Ramadan), hajj with sacrificial slaughter, and *īmān* (faith) with jihad."

[6]

ʿAbdullāh ibn al-Mubārak said, "The one who prays twelve *rakʿah*s everyday has fulfilled the right of prayer; the one who fasts three days every month has fulfilled the right of fasting; the one who recites one hundred verses everyday has fulfilled the right of the Qur'an; and the one who gives a dirham in charity every Friday has fulfilled the right of charity."

[7]

ʿUmar ﷺ said, "There are four types of oceans - passion is the ocean of sins, the nafs is the ocean of desires, death is the ocean of lives, and the grave is the ocean of regrets."

[8]

ʿUthmān ﷺ said, "I found the sweetness of worship in four things - the first in fulfilling Allah's commandments, the second in abstaining from Allah's prohibitions, the third in enjoining good with the intention of attaining Allah's reward of Allah, and the fourth in forbidding evil fearing Allah's wrath."

[9]

'Uthmān ⬥ also said, "There are four things, the outward of which is a virtue but the inner of which is an obligation – being in the company of the righteous is a virtue and imitating them is an obligation; reciting the Qur'an is a virtue and acting according to its commandments is an obligation; visiting the graves is a virtue and preparing for the time when one will enter them is an obligation; visiting a sick person is a virtue and asking him for advice is an obligation."

[10]

'Alī ⬥ said, "The one who longs for Paradise will rush towards good deeds; the one who dreads Hell will put an end to his vices; the one who has a firm conviction in [the imminent arrival of] death will lose all his passions; and the one who really knows the *dunyā* will find disasters easy to bear."

[11]

It is said that Allah revealed to one of the prophets of Banī Isrā'īl: "Remaining silent instead of speaking evil is fasting for Me; guarding your organs against prohibitions is prayer for Me; losing any hope in creatures [that they can bring one good or evil] is charity for Me; and refraining from hurting Muslims is jihad for Me."

[12]

'Abdullāh ibn Mas'ūd ⬥ said, "Four things are from the darkness of the heart – a full stomach without caring [whether it is *ḥalāl* or *ḥarām*]; keeping the company of oppressors; forgetting past sins; and being under the delusion that one's lifetime will surely be long. There are another four things that are from the illumination of the heart – an empty stomach because of caution; accompanying the righteous; remembering past sins; and not expecting to live for long."

[13]

Ḥātim al-Aṣamm said, "The one who claims four things without doing four others has lied - the one who claims to love Allah yet does not abstain from things prohibited by Him has lied; the one who claims to love the Prophet ﷺ yet dislikes the poor and needy has lied; the one who claims to love Paradise yet does not give charity has lied; and the one who claims to fear Hell yet does not give up sinning has lied."

[14]

The Prophet ﷺ said, "Premonitory signs of wretchedness are four - forgetting past sins whilst their record is with Allah the Exalted; remembering past good deeds whilst one does not know whether they have been accepted or rejected; looking to those of a higher status in the *dunyā*; and looking to those of a lower status in the Religion [of Islam]. Allah will say, 'I wanted him but he did not want Me and thus I have left him.' Premonitory signs of bliss are four - remembering past sins; forgetting past good deeds; looking at those of a higher status in the Religion [of Islam]; and looking at those of a lower status in the *dunyā*."

[15]

A sage once said, "The rites of faith (*īmān*) are four - God-consciousness, shame, gratitude and patience."

[16]

The Prophet ﷺ said, "Mothers are four: the mother of cures, the mother of manners, the mother of worship, and the mother of hopes. The mother of cures is eating less, the mother of manners is speaking less, the mother of worship is sinning less, and the mother of hopes is patience."

[17]

The Prophet ﷺ also said, "There are four gems in the body of the son of Adam that are removed by four things - as for the gems they are intellect, Religion, shame, and good deeds. Anger removes the intellect, envy removes Religion, desire removes shame, and backbiting removes good deeds."

[18]

He ﷺ also said, "There are four things in Paradise that are better than Paradise itself - remaining eternally in Paradise is better than Paradise; being served by the angels in Paradise is better than Paradise; being in the company of the Prophets in Paradise is better than Paradise; and gaining Allah's pleasure in Paradise is better than Paradise itself. There are four things in Hell that are worse than Hell itself - remaining eternally in Hell is worse than Hell; the reproaching of the unbelievers by the angels in Hell is worse than Hell; being in the company of Satan in Hell is worse than Hell; and Allah's wrath in Hell is worse than Hell itself."

[19]

When one of the sages was asked, "How are you?" He replied, "I am with my Lord in compliance, with the nafs in opposition, with creatures in [giving and taking] advice, and with the *dunyā* only in necessity."

[20]

A sage selected four aphorisms from the four revealed Books - from the Torah: "The one who is content with what Allah has given him will find repose in this world and in the next"; from the Bible: "The one who destroys his vices will be honoured in this world and in the next"; from the Psalms: "The one who isolates himself away from people will find salvation in this world and in the next"; and from the Qur'an, "The one who safeguards his tongue will be safe in this world and in the next."

[21]

ʿUmar ﷺ said, "I swear by Allah! I have never been tested by hardship except that Allah bestowed upon me due to it four blessings - the first is that I was not tested through a sin; the second, that the hardship was not greater than it was; the third, I wasn't deprived of being contented with it; the fourth, I hope that I will be rewarded for it."

[22]

ʿAbdullāh ibn al-Mubārak said, "A wise man collected numerous sayings and from them he selected forty thousand; from the forty thousand he selected four thousand, from the four thousand he selected four hundred, from the four hundred he selected forty, and from the forty he selected four - the first, "Don't trust a woman in any situation"; the second, "Don't be deluded by wealth in any situation"; the third, "Don't burden your stomach with what it can't bear"; and the fourth, "Don't gather from knowledge that which is of no benefit to you."

[23]

Commenting on Allah's saying in the Qur'an, "Then the angels called to him as he stood praying in the sanctuary: That Allah gives you the good news of Yaḥyā verifying a Word from Allah; a master, a chaste man, and a prophet from among the righteous," Muḥammad ibn Aḥmad said, "Allah described Prophet Yaḥyā as a 'master' despite being His slave because he had overpowered four things - passion, Satan, the tongue, and anger."

[24]

ʿAlī ﷺ said, "*Dīn* and *dunyā* will continue to exist as long as four things exist - as long as the rich are not miserly in that with which they have been blessed; as long as scholars practise what they have learnt; as long as the ignorant are not arrogant about that which they do not know; and as long as the poor do not sell the Hereafter in return for the *dunyā*."

[25]

The Prophet ﷺ said, "On the Day of Judgement Allah will use four people as a proof against four types of people - [Prophet] Sulaymān (Solomon) against the rich, [Prophet] Yūsuf against servants, [Prophet] Ayyūb against the sick, and [Prophet] ʿĪsā (Jesus) against the poor."

[26]

Saᶜd ibn Bilāl said, "Despite committing a sin, Allah still bestows four blessings on His sinful servant - He does not cut off his sustenance, He does not cause his health to deteriorate, He does not make the sin apparent on him for all to see, and He does not hasten his punishment."

[27]

Ḥātim al-Aṣamm said, "The one who delays four things until four others will find Paradise - sleep until the grave, pride until after the accounting [of good and bad deeds], repose until after the crossing of the *sirāṭ* (bridge to be crossed on the Day of Judgement), and desires until entering Paradise."

[28]

Ḥāmid al-Laffāf said, "We searched for four things in four others and failed to find them there, but found them in yet another four things - we sought richness in money but found it in contentment; we sought peace in opulence but found it in poverty; we sought pleasure in abundance but found it in good health; and we sought sustenance in the earth and found it in the sky."

[29]

ᶜAlī ﵁ said, "Four things, a little of which is still a lot - pain, poverty, fire, and enmity."

[30]

Ḥātim al-Aṣamm said, "Four things are not appreciated except by four types of people - youth is not appreciated but by the old, freedom from worries is not appreciated but by those afflicted with calamities, health is not appreciated but by those in poor health, and life is not appreciated but by the dead."

[31]

The poet Abū Nuwwās said:

My sins, if I think about them, are many
But the mercy of my Lord is much vaster
I do not hope for salvation in any good action I may have done
Rather in Allah's mercy is my hope
He is Allah my Lord who is my Creator
And I am [in front of Him] a slave who obeys and submits
If forgiveness is intended for me then that is mercy
And if it is other than it then what am I to do?

[32]

The Prophet ﷺ said, "On the Day of Judgement the Scales will be placed and the people of prayer will be brought forward and they will be compensated according to the Scales; then the people of fasting will be brought forward and they will be compensated according to the Scales; then the people of hajj will be brought forward and they will be compensated according to the Scales; and then the people afflicted with hardships and calamities [in the *dunyā*] will be brought forward and the Scales will not be used for them nor will their records be brought out, and they will be given their reward without any account, so much so that the people who used to be free of worries and calamities would wish that they were in their position, such is the immensity of their reward from Allah the Exalted."

[33]

A wise man said, "The son of Adam will face four seizures - the Angel of Death will seize his soul, his heirs will seize his wealth, the worms will seize his body, and his adversaries (the people he had wronged or backbitten) will seize his honour, meaning his good deeds, on the Day of Judgement."

[34]

A sage said, "The one who preoccupies himself with desires must have women; the one who preoccupies himself with collecting wealth must indulge in the prohibited; the one who preoccupies himself with bringing benefit to Muslims must have secrecy; and the one who preoccupies himself with worship must have knowledge."

[35]

ʿAlī ؓ said, "The most difficult of actions are four - forgiving when in a state of anger, contentment in times of hardship, chastity in seclusion, and speaking the truth in front of someone whom one fears or from whom one hopes for largesse."

[36]

In the Psalms it is stated, "Allah revealed to [Prophet] Dāwūd that a wise and intelligent person never neglects four periods of time - a time to intimately converse with his Lord, a time to bring himself to account, a time to visit those of his brothers who will show him his defects, and a time to give himself free reign to indulge in the permissible."

[37]

A sage once said, "The whole of worship is in four things - honouring promises, abiding by the limits [set by Divine Law], being patient over loss, and being content with whatever is in one's possession."

4

Counsel in Fives

[1]

The Prophet ﷺ was reported to have said, "The one who mocks five will lose five - the one who mocks scholars will lose his Religion (*dīn*); the one who mocks rulers will lose this life (*dunyā*); the one who mocks his neighbours will lose their assistance; the one who mocks the strong and mighty will lose their compassion; and the one who mocks his family will lose the joy of living."

[2]

The Prophet ﷺ said, "There will come a time for my *ummah* when they will love five things and forget five things - they will love this life (*dunyā*) and forget the life to come; they will love property and forget the grave; they will love wealth and forget the [Day of] Judgement; they will love their children and forget the truth; and they will love themselves and forget Allah. They have nothing to do with me and I have nothing to do with them."

[3]

The Prophet ﷺ said, "Allah does not give someone five things until

He has prepared another five things for him - He does not give him gratitude except that He has prepared for him an increase [in provision and sustenance], He does not give him supplication (*duʿāʾ*) except that He has prepared its award; He does not give him the asking for forgiveness (*istighfār*) except that He has prepared for him forgiveness; He does not give him the asking for repentance except that He has prepared for him acceptance; and He does not give him charity except that He has prepared for him its reward."

[4]

Abū Bakr al-Ṣiddīq ﷺ said, "Darkness is of five types and its lamps are five - love of the *dunyā* is a darkness and its lamp is God-consciousness; sins are a darkness and their lamp is repentance; the grave is a darkness and its lamp is: 'There is no god but Allah, Muḥammad is the Messenger of Allah'; the Hereafter is a darkness and its lamp is righteous actions; and the path is a darkness and its lamp is certitude."

[5]

ʿUmar ﷺ said, "If it were not claiming to know the unseen, I would bear witness that these five types of people will surely be from the people of Paradise - the poor man who has to support a large family; the wife whose husband is pleased with her; the woman who gives her dowry to her husband, considering it an act of charity; the one whose parents are pleased with him; and the one who repents from sins."

[6]

ʿUthmān ﷺ said, "The signs of a God-conscious person are five - the first is that he does not sit except with someone who is concerned for the Religion and has control over his sexual desires and tongue; if a great fortune befalls him from the *dunyā* he deems it a trial; if he finds a practice to be from the Religion he clings to it, though it may seem insignificant; he does not fill his stomach with the *ḥalāl* fearing that *ḥarām* may be mixed with it; and he supposes that all of the people will be saved and that his soul will perish."

[7]

ʿAlī ﷺ said, "Were it not for five things all of mankind would have been righteous - contentment with ignorance, covetousness over this world (*dunyā*), miserliness over what is surplus, insincerity in actions, and conceit over one's opinion."

[8]

ʿAbdullāh ibn ʿAmr ibn al-ʿĀṣ, may Allah be pleased with him and his father, said, "Five things, he who embodies them will be happy in this world and in the next - the first is to regularly say, *'Lā ilāha illā Allah, Muḥammadun rasūlu Allah'* - There is no god but Allah, Muḥammad is the Messenger of Allah; the second is to say when inflicted with a calamity, *'Innā lillāhi wa innā ilayhi rājiʿūn, wa lā ḥawla wa lā quwwata illā billāhil ʿalīyyil ʿaẓīm'* - Verily we belong to Allah and to Him we shall all return, and there is no power or might except by the will of Allah the most High, the Mighty; the third is to say in gratitude when given a blessing, *'Al-ḥamdu lillāhi rabbil ʿālamīn'* - Praise be to Allah, Lord of the Universe; the fourth is to say when beginning anything, *'Bismillāhir raḥmānir raḥīm'* - In the name of Allah the most Merciful the most Kind; and the fifth is to say upon committing a sin, *'Astaghfiru llāhal ʿaẓīma wa atūbu ilayh'* - I seek the forgiveness of Allah the Greatest and I repent to Him."

[9]

Al-Ḥasan al-Baṣrī said, "In the Torah are written five lessons - wealth is in contentment, safety is in seclusion, dignity is in rejecting desires, enjoyment is in long days (in the Hereafter), and patience is in a few days (in the *dunyā*)."

[10]

The Prophet ﷺ said, "Make use of five before five - your youth before your old age, your health before your sickness, your wealth before your poverty, your life before your death, and your free time before your preoccupation."

[11]

Yaḥyā ibn Muᶜādh al-Rāzī said, "He whose appetite increases, his corpulence will increase; he whose corpulence increases, his desires will increase; he whose desires increase, his sins will increase; he whose sins increase, the hardness of his heart will increase; and he whose heart becomes hard will drown in the pitfalls of the *dunyā* and its attractions."

[12]

Sufyān al-Thawrī said, "The poor have chosen five things and the rich have chosen five others - the poor have chosen serenity of the soul, freedom from worries, worship of the Lord, ease of accountability, and the highest position. The rich have chosen weariness of the soul, preoccupation with worries, worship of the *dunyā*, severity in accountability, and the lowest position."

[13]

ᶜAbdullāh al-Anṭākī said: "Five things are from the remedies of the heart - sitting with the righteous, reading the Qur'an, emptiness of the stomach, standing at night [in prayer], and supplicating at dawn."

[14]

The majority of the scholars have agreed that, "Contemplation is of five types - contemplating Allah's signs results in affirming the oneness of Allah (*tawḥīd*) and in conviction; contemplating Allah's blessings results in loving Allah; contemplating Allah's promise [of reward and paradise for the good-doers] results in creating a desire to do good; contemplating Allah's punishment results in fear and awe of Him; and contemplating one's shortcomings in obedience despite Allah's blessings and mercy towards oneself results in a sense of shame and humility."

[15]

A sage said, "There are five obstacles to attaining God-consciousness (*taqwā*), and only the one who overcomes these five will attain it -

choosing hardship over ease, exertion over rest, lowliness over pride, silence over idle talk, and death over life."

[16]
The Prophet ﷺ said, "Discreetness safeguards secrets, charity safeguards wealth, sincerity safeguards good deeds, truthfulness safeguards speech, and consultation safeguards opinions."

[17]
The Prophet ﷺ said, "In the gathering of wealth there are five [blameworthy] things - wearing oneself out in gathering it; neglecting the remembrance (*dhikr*) of Allah in preserving it; fear of robbers and thieves; being labelled a miser on account of it; and leaving the company of the righteous due to it. In distributing one's wealth to the poor there are five [praiseworthy] things - ease of mind due to abandoning its amassing; having time to remember Allah rather than worrying about preserving it; safety from robbers and thieves; gaining the title of 'generous'; and accompanying the righteous due to leaving it behind."

[18]
Sufyān al-Thawrī said, "No one in this age amasses wealth except that he has five traits - the delusion that his lifespan will be long, overpowering greed, intense miserliness, lack of piety, and forgetfulness of the Hereafter."

[19]
A poet said:

O you who seeks the hand of the *dunyā* in marriage! Know that she has a new lover everyday
She takes a husband now, yet gives herself at the same time to another elsewhere
She only accepts lovers so that she may kill them in her bosom one by one
I have been fooled and the affliction is spreading in my body little by little
Ready yourself and take provisions for death, for the herald has

called: 'tis time to leave, 'tis time to leave!

[20]

Ḥātim al-Aṣamm said, "Hastiness is from Satan except in five situations in which it is the *sunnah* of the Messenger of Allah to hasten - feeding the guest when he arrives; preparing the deceased for burial when he dies; marrying off the daughters when they reach the age of maturity; paying a debt when it is due; and making repentance from a sin as soon as it is committed."

[21]

Muḥammad ibn al-Dūrī said, "The damnation of Iblīs was due to five things - he did not acknowledge his sin, he did not regret it, he did not blame himself, he did not resolve to repent, and he lost hope in the mercy of Allah. The salvation of Adam was due to five things - he acknowledged his sin, he regretted it, he blamed himself, he hastened to repent, and he did not lose hope in the mercy of Allah."

[22]

Shaqīq al-Balkhī said, "Five precepts are obligatory upon you, so practise them - worship Allah to the extent that you need Him; take from the *dunyā* to the extent of your stay in it; disobey Allah to the extent that you can bear His punishment; prepare provisions during the *dunyā* to the extent of your stay in the grave; and work for Paradise to the extent of your desired rank in it."

[23]

ʿUmar ﵁ said: 'I have seen all types of friends but I never found a friend better than safeguarding the tongue; I have seen all types of clothes but I never found clothes better than God-consciousness; I have seen all types of wealth but I never found wealth better than contentment; I have seen all types of good deeds but I never found a good deed better than giving good advice; and I have seen all types of food and I never found food more delicious than patience."

[24]

A sage said, "Asceticism (*zuhd*) is in five things - confidence in Allah, independence from creatures, sincerity in actions, bearing oppression, and contentment with what one has in his hand."

[25]

During some of his supplications and entreaties, a devotee said, "O my Lord! Thinking that my lifespan will be long has deluded me, love of the *dunyā* has destroyed me, Satan has misled me, the nafs that inclines to evil prevented me from abiding by the truth, my wicked companion helped me in disobedience, so save me O Helper of those who seek help! If You do not have mercy on me then who will?"

[26]

The Prophet ﷺ said, "There will come a time for my *ummah* when they will love five things and forget five others - they will love this world (*dunyā*) and forget the next world; they will love life and forget death; they will love palaces and forget the grave; they will love wealth and forget the [Day of] Account; and they will love creatures and forget the Creator."

[27]

Yaḥyā ibn Muʿādh al-Rāzī said in his entreaties and supplication, "O my Lord! The night is only pleasant to me when I supplicate to You; the day is only pleasant to me when I obey You; this world is only pleasant to me when I remember You; the Hereafter will only be pleasant to me if I receive Your pardon; and Paradise will only be pleasant to me if I see You."

5

Counsel in Sixes

[1]

The Prophet ﷺ said, "Six things are strangers in six situations - the mosque is a stranger amongst people who do not pray; the Qur'an is a stranger in a household where it is not read; the memorised Qur'an is a stranger in the heart of an open sinner (*fāsiq*); a righteous Muslim woman is a stranger in the hands of an oppressive husband of bad character; a pious Muslim man is a stranger in the hands of an evil wife of bad character; and a scholar is a stranger amongst a group of people who do not listen to him." Then he said, "Verily Allah the Exalted will not look at them on the Day of Judgement in a merciful manner."

[2]

The Prophet ﷺ said, "There are six [types of] people whom I have cursed and Allah has cursed, for the supplication of every Prophet is accepted - He who adds anything to the Book of Allah; he who disbelieves in the decree of Allah the Exalted; he who oppressively uses his power to elevate those whom Allah has brought low and to bring low those whom Allah has elevated; he who publicly disobeys Allah's commandments; he who makes lawful that which is unlawful; and he who leaves my *Sunnah* (Tradition) - Allah the Exalted will not look at them on the Day of Judgement in a merciful manner."

[3]

Abū Bakr al-Ṣiddīq ⬥ said, "Iblīs is standing in front of you, your nafs is on your right, your desire is on your left, the *dunyā* is behind you, your limbs and senses are around you, and the Omnipotent is above you. Iblīs, may Allah curse him, calls you to leave the Religion (*dīn*), the nafs calls you to disobedience, desire calls you to [fulfilling your] passions, the *dunyā* calls you to choose it over the Hereafter, your limbs and senses call you towards sins, and the Omnipotent calls you to Paradise and forgiveness. Allah the Exalted says [in the Qur'an], "And Allah invites you to Paradise and forgiveness." The one who responds to Iblīs will lose his Religion, the one responds to the nafs will lose his soul, the one who responds to desire will lose his intellect, the one who responds to the *dunyā* will lose the Hereafter, the one who responds to his limbs and senses will lose Paradise, and the one who responds to Allah will lose all his sins and acquire all types of goodness."

[4]

ʿUmar ⬥ said, "Allah has concealed six things in six others - He has concealed pleasure in obedience, anger in disobedience, His Greatest Name in the Qur'an, the Night of Power (*laylatul qadr*) in Ramadan, the Middle Prayer (*al-ṣalātul wusṭā*) amongst the prayers, and the Day of Judgement amongst the days."

[5]

ʿUthmān ⬥ said, "The believer is in six types of fear - the first is that Allah the Exalted will take away his *īmān* (faith); the second is that the angels will write down things that will expose him on the Day of Judgement; the third is that Satan will render his actions void; the fourth is that the Angel of Death will take his soul when he is in a state of heedlessness; the fifth is that the *dunyā* will delude him and make him work for other than the Hereafter; and the sixth is that his family and children will preoccupy him such that he neglects the remembrance of Allah the Exalted."

[6]

ʿAlī 🕮 said, "The one who gathers six traits will not have left anything that brings him closer to Paradise or anything that makes him escape Hell - he came to know Allah the Exalted and thus obeyed him; he came to know Satan and thus disobeyed him; he came to know the Hereafter and thus sought it; he came to know the *dunyā* and thus rejected it; he came to know the Truth and thus followed it; and he came to know falsehood and thus steered clear of it."

[7]

ʿAlī 🕮 also said, "Blessings are six - Islam, the Qur'an, Muḥammad - the Messenger of Allah 🕮, well-being, Allah's protection, and nondependence on people."

[8]

Yaḥyā ibn Muʿādh al-Rāzī said, "Knowledge is the proof of action, comprehension is the vessel of knowledge, the intellect is the leader to goodness, desire is the mount of sins, wealth is the garment of the arrogant, and this world is the market for the next world."

[9]

Abū Dharr Jimhir said, "Six things equal everything in the *dunyā* - satisfying food, a virtuous child, a sensible wife, wise speech, a mature intellect, and a healthy body."

[10]

Al-Ḥasan al-Baṣrī said, "Were it not for saints, the earth and everything in it would have been destroyed; were it not for the virtuous, the corrupt would have perished; were it not for scholars, people would have become like cattle; were it not for rulers, people would have killed one another; were it not for fools, the *dunyā* would have been devastated out of neglect; and were it not for the wind, everything would have stagnated."

[11]

A sage said, "The one who does not fear Allah will not be safe from the lapses of the tongue; the heart of one who does not fear meeting Allah will be safe neither from unlawful (*ḥarām*) things, nor from things over the permissibility of which there is doubt; the one who does not break off dependence on creatures will not be safe from greed; the one who does not safeguard [the sincerity of] his actions will not be safe from showing-off; the one who does not seek the help of Allah in guarding his heart will not be safe from jealousy; and the one who does not look to those who are better than him in knowledge and worship will not be safe from pride."

[12]

Al-Ḥasan al-Baṣrī said, "The corruption of people's hearts is in six things - the first is that they sin with the hope of repentance; they seek knowledge but do not act upon it; if they do act upon it they are insincere in doing so; they eat the sustenance Allah has provided them but do not show gratitude for it; they are not content with the allotment (*qisma*) of Allah; and they bury their dead but do not take heed."

[13]

Al-Ḥasan al-Baṣrī also said, "Allah will inflict six punishments on the one who loves the *dunyā* and chooses it over Hereafter - three in this world and three in the next. As for the three in this world they are - delusion and hope in having a long lifetime that has no end, overpowering greed that leaves no contentment, and the taking away of the sweetness of worship. As for the three in the Hereafter they are - the harrowing ordeal of the Day of Judgement, a severe bringing to account, and an eternal regret."

[14]

Aḥnaf ibn Qays said, "There is no rest for the envious; there is no moral integrity for the liar; there is no well-being for the miser; there is no loyalty for kings; there is no nobility for the ill-mannered; there is no abrogation for Allah's decree."

[15]

Some sages were asked, "When a servant [of Allah] repents, how does he know whether his repentance has been accepted or rejected?" They said, "We can't pass a judgement in this matter, but there are indications that the repentance has been accepted - that he does not deem himself immune from disobedience; that he sees happiness absent from his heart and sadness ever-present therein; that he draws close to the people of virtue and moves far from the people of disobedience; that he sees little from this *dunyā* as much and the many good deeds he's done for the Hereafter as little; that he sees his heart busy with that which he wishes to secure from Allah the Exalted [i.e. Paradise] and empty of concern for that which Allah the Exalted had already secured for him [i.e. his daily sustenance]; that he safeguards his tongue and is ever contemplative in a state of continuous remorse and regret."

[16]

Yaḥyā ibn Muʿādh said, "From the greatest of all delusions in my sight is - the continuance in acts of disobedience in the hope of forgiveness without any regret; expecting nearness to Allah without performing any acts of obedience; waiting to reap the crop of Paradise having sown the seeds of Hell; seeking to reside in the House of the obedient ones [i.e. Paradise] with acts of disobedience; waiting for reward without meriting it with deeds; and excessive hope in the kindness of Allah the Exalted with heedlessness:

They hope for salvation without treading its path
Surely a ship does not sail on solid ground."

[17]

Aḥnaf ibn Qays was asked, "What is the best thing that can be given to a servant [of Allah]?" He replied, "An instinctively upright intellect." It was said, "And if not this?" He said, "Good manners." It was said, "And if not this?" He said, "An agreeable companion." It was said, "And if not this?" He said. "A heart attached [to Allah]." It was said, "And if not this." He said, "Long silence." It was said, "And if not this?" He said, "Immediate death."

6

Counsel in Sevens

[1]

Abū Hurayra ﵁ narrated that the Prophet ﷺ said, "Seven [types of] people are shaded by Allah in the shade of His Throne, on the Day when there will be no shade but His Shade [i.e. on the Day of Judgement] - a just ruler, a young man who grew up in the worship of Allah, a person whose heart is attached to the mosque [and longs to return to it] from the moment he leaves it until he returns to it, two persons who love each other for the sake of Allah, meet for His sake and depart from each other for His sake, a person who remembers Allah in solitude and his eyes well up with tears, a man whom an extremely beautiful and rich woman seduces, but he [rejecting her seduction] says, 'I fear Allah'; and a person who gives charity and conceals it [to such an extent] that his left hand does not know what his right hand has given."

[2]

Abū Bakr al-Ṣiddīq ﵁ said, "The miser will not escape one of seven things - either he will die and the one who will inherit his wealth will spend it in that which Allah the Exalted has forbidden, or Allah will empower over him a tyrant ruler who will take his wealth from him after humiliating him, or He will inflame in him a desire that will cause him to lose his wealth, or he will have the idea of constructing a building in an unsuitable piece of land and will thus waste his wealth, or one of the calamities of the *dunyā* such as drowning, burning, theft or similar things will befall it, or he will be afflicted with a permanent illness and he will spend all his wealth seeking a cure, or he will bury the wealth in a place which he will forget and thus will never find it again."

[3]

ʿUmar ﷺ said, "The one who laughs a lot will lose his respect; the one who makes mockery of people will be mocked by others; the one who is excessive in something will become known by it; the one who speaks a lot will make many blunders; the one who makes many blunders will lose his sense of shame; the one who loses his sense of shame will lose his God-consciousness; and the one who loses his God-consciousness will cause his heart to die."

[4]

ʿUthmān ﷺ said when discussing the saying of Allah the Exalted, "And beneath it was a treasure for them, and their father was a righteous man", "the treasure is a gold tablet and on it were written seven lines: 'I am amazed at the one who knows death is coming yet laughs; I am amazed at the one who knows that the *dunyā* will perish yet pursues it; I am amazed at the one who knows that all things are predestined yet becomes distressed over what he has missed; I am amazed at the one who knows about accountability and yet gathers wealth; I am amazed at the one who knows about the Hellfire yet sins; I am amazed at the one who believes in Allah with certainty yet remembers others beside Him; I am amazed at the one who believes in Paradise with certainty yet is at ease in the *dunyā*; and I am amazed at the one who knows Satan is an enemy yet obeys him.'"

[5]

ᶜAlī ﷺ was asked, "What is heavier than the sky? What is wider than the earth? What is richer than the sea? What is harder than rock? What is hotter than fire? What is colder than ice? What is more bitter than poison?" He replied, "Accusing the innocent is heavier than the sky; the Truth is wider than the earth; a content heart is richer than the sea; the heart of a hypocrite is harder than rock; a tyrant ruler is hotter that fire; being in need of help from a scoundrel is colder than ice; and patience is more bitter than poison (and in another narration, backbiting is more bitter than poison)."

[6]

The Prophet said ﷺ, "The *dunyā* is home for the one who has no home, and wealth for the one who has no wealth. Only the one who has no intellect gathers for it; only the one who has no comprehension acts according to its desires; only the one who has no knowledge will be punished for it; only the one who has no intellect will become jealous for it; and only the one who has no conviction strives for it."

[7]

Jābir ibn ᶜAbdullāh al-Anṣārī ﷺ narrated that the Prophet ﷺ said, "Jibrā'īl used to remind me of the rights of the neighbour to such an extent that I thought a neighbour will be given the right to inherit from his neighbour; he used to remind me of the rights of women to such an extent that I thought that divorcing them would be made forbidden; he used to remind me of the rights of slaves to such an extent that I thought there will be a time fixed when they will be freed; he used to remind me of the use of *siwāk* (tooth-stick) to such an extent that I thought it would be made obligatory; he used to remind me of the importance of prayer in congregation to such an extent that I thought that Allah the Exalted will not accept prayer except in congregation; he used to remind me about standing up in the night and praying to such an extent that I thought that there will be no sleep during the night; and he used to remind me about the remembrance of Allah to such an extent that I thought there is no benefit in any speech except in it."

[8]

The Prophet ﷺ said, "There are seven people whom the Creator will neither look at on the Day of Judgement nor will He purify them, and He will make them enter the Hellfire - the homosexual and his partner; the one who masturbates; the one who engages in bestiality; the one who has anal intercourse with a woman; a man who marries both a woman and her daughter; the one who fornicates with his neighbour's wife; and the one who hurts his neighbour to such a degree that he curses him."

[9]

The Prophet ﷺ said, "The martyrs are seven apart from those killed in the way of Allah - the one who dies of an internal hemorrhage is a martyr, the one who dies from drowning is a martyr, pleurisy is a martyr, the one who dies in a fire is a martyr, the one who dies under a collapsed building is a martyr, and the woman who dies when giving birth is a martyr."

[10]

Ibn ᶜAbbās ؓ said, "It is a duty on an intelligent person to choose seven things over seven others - poverty over wealth, lowliness over honour, humility over arrogance, hunger over satiety, sadness over happiness, inferiority over superiority, and death over life."

7

Counsel in Eights

[1]

The Prophet ﷺ said, "Eight things are never satiated of eight - the eye from looking, the earth from rain, the female from the male, the scholar from knowledge, the questioner from questioning, the greedy from gathering, the sea from water, and fire from wood."

[2]

Abū Bakr al-Ṣiddīq ؓ said, "There are eight things which are adorn-ments for eight others - chastity is the adornment for poverty; grati-tude is the adornment for blessings; patience is the adornment for calamity; gentleness is the adornment for knowledge; humility is the adornment for the student; much crying is the adornment for fear [of Allah]; not boasting of one's generosity to its recipient is the adorn-ment for charity; and complete calmness and inner concentration is the adornment for prayer."

[3]

ʿUmar ؓ said, "The one who abandons superfluous speech will be given wisdom; the one who abandons superfluous looking will be given the tranquillity of the heart; the one who abandons superfluous food will be given delight in worship; the one who abandons superfluous laughter will be given veneration; the one who abandons superfluous joking will be given a beautiful appearance; the one who abandons the love of the *dunyā* will be granted the love of the Hereafter; the one who abandons busying himself with the faults of others will be given the ability to rectify his own faults; and the one who abandons questioning the Essence of Allah the Exalted will be given security from hypocrisy."

[4]

ʿUthmān ﵁ said, "Signs of a person who really know Allah are eight - his heart is in a state of fear and hope, his tongue is in a state of praise and gratitude, his eyes are in a state of shame and tears, and his will is in leaving the *dunyā* and seeking the pleasure of his Lord.

[5]

ʿAlī ﵁ said, "There is no good in prayer without concentration and calmness; there is no good in fasting without refraining from idle talk; there is no good in reading without any contemplation; there is no good in knowledge without piety; there is no good in wealth without generosity; there is no good in brotherhood without caring for one another; there is no good in a blessing that is short-lived; and there is no good in supplication without sincerity."

8

Counsel in Nines

[1]

The Prophet ﷺ said, "Allah the Exalted revealed to Mūsā ibn ᶜImrān (Moses) in the Torah that the source of all mistakes are three - arrogance, envy and greed. Another six diseases were born out of these three, and thus they became nine - satiety, excessive sleep, excessive rest, love of wealth, love of praise, and love of leadership."

[2]

Abū Bakr al-Ṣiddīq ؓ said, "Worshippers are of three groups, each group has three signs by which it is known - a group who worship Allah the Exalted out of fear; a group who worship Allah out of hope; and a group who worship Allah out of love. For the first group there are three signs - they disparage themselves; deem their righteous deeds to be few; and their evil deeds to be plenty. For the second group there are three signs - They are an example to others in all situations; they are the most generous of all people in spending their wealth; and they have the best of opinion amongst creatures regarding Allah. As for the third group there are three signs - they give away what they love most and do not care as long as their Lord is pleased with them; and they do that which will displease their nafs to please their Lord; and they are with their Lord in every situation, whether it be in [following] His commandments or [avoiding] His prohibitions."

[3]

ʿUmar said, "The progeny of Satan are nine - Zalītūn, Wathīn, Laqūs, Aʿwān, Haffāf, Murra, al-Musawwiṭ, Dāsim and Walhān. Zalītūn commands the markets and he unfurls his banner therein; Wathīn commands catastrophes; Aʿwān commands rulers; Haffāf commands intoxicants; Murra commands licentious music; Laqūs commands the Magians; Al-Musawwiṭ commands [false] news which he puts in the mouths of people while they know not its origin; Dāsim commands houses: if a man were to enter his house without greeting his wife and family with salām and mentioning the name of Allah the Exalted, Dāsim will cause a dispute between husband and wife such that it leads to divorce, separation, or violence; as for Walhān, he whispers [in people's ears] during ablution, prayer, and other acts of worship."

[4]

ʿUthmān said, "The one who observes the five daily prayers in their proper times and is constant in this, Allah will honour him with nine miracles - Allah will love him, his health will be good, angels will protect him, blessedness (*baraka*) will descend on his house, the sign of the righteous will be apparent on his face, Allah will soften his heart, he will cross the bridge of *al-sirāṭ al-mustaqīm* [in the Hereafter] at the speed of a flash of lightning, Allah will save him from Hellfire, and Allah will place him amongst the people who have no fear nor are they ever sad."

[5]

ʿAlī said, "Shedding tears is of three types - the first is from the fear of Allah's punishment, the second is from the fear of Allah's anger, and the third is from the fear of being cut off from Allah. The first one is a compensation for sins, the second is purification from faults, and the third is elevation to the ranks of sainthood accompanied by the pleasure of the Beloved. The fruit of the compensation of sins is salvation from punishment; the fruit of the purification of faults is eternal bliss and high ranks; and the fruit of the elevation to the ranks of sainthood accompanied by the pleasure of the Beloved is glad tidings from Allah the Exalted of His pleasure, of seeing Him, of the visiting of angels, and of an increase in virtue."

9

Counsel in Tens

[1]

The Messenger of Allah ﷺ said, "Use the *siwāk*, for there are ten benefits in it - it purifies the mouth, pleases the Lord, angers Satan, is loved by the Merciful and by the guardian angels, strengthens the gums, eliminates phlegm, gets rid of the bad taste from the mouth, brightens the eyes, eliminates bad breath, and is from my *sunnah*." He then added, "One prayer after [using] the *siwāk* is better than seventy prayers without [using] it."

[2]

Abū Bakr al-Ṣiddīq ﷻ said, "There is not a servant whom Allah has given the following ten traits except that he will be saved from all pitfalls and afflictions, reach the rank of those who are close to Allah, and attain the position of the pious ones - the first is perpetual truthfulness together with a content heart; the second, complete patience together with permanent gratitude; the third, perpetual poverty together with ever-present asceticism (*zuhd*); the fourth, uninterrupted contemplation together with an empty stomach; the fifth, lasting sadness together with continuous fear; the sixth, perpetual struggle together with a humble body; the seventh, perpetual gentleness together with ever-present mercy; the eighth, perpetual love [of Allah] together with shame; the ninth, beneficial knowledge together with perpetual patience; and the tenth, perpetual faith (*īmān*) with an unflappable intellect."

[3]

ʿUmar ؓ said, "Ten things are not right without ten others - intelligence without God-consciousness, superiority without knowledge, success without fear, power without justice, noble lineage without manners, happiness without security, wealth without generosity, poverty without contentment, [having] a high and exalted position without humility, and jihad without the guidance and support of Allah."

[4]

ʿUthmān ؓ said, "The most futile of all things are ten - a scholar who is not asked, knowledge which is not acted upon, a correct opinion which is not accepted, a weapon which is not used, a mosque wherein none pray, a copy of the Qur'an which is not read, wealth which is not spent, a horse which is not mounted, knowledge of asceticism by one who pursues the *dunyā*, and a long life in which no provisions have been prepared for the departure."

[5]

ʿAlī ؓ said, "Knowledge is the best inheritance, good manners are the best craft, piety is the best provision, worship is the best baggage, righteous action is the best guide, good character is the best companion, gentleness is the best adviser, contentment is the best wealth, [divine] assistance is the best ally, and death is the best teacher."

[6]

The Messenger of Allah ﷺ said, "Ten [types of people] from this *um-*

mah are disbelievers (*kuffār*) in Allah the Great and who think they are believers - the killer without a right, the one who practices magic, the withholder of *zakāt*, the drinker of alcohol, the one upon whom hajj became obligatory but did not perform it, the spreader of sedition and trouble (*fitna*), the seller of weapons to the enemy, the one who has anal intercourse with a woman, the one who commits adultery with a close female relative (*maḥram*) whom he is legally forbidden to marry - if they deem what they have done permissible (*ḥalāl*) then they have apostatised."

[7]

The Messenger of Allah ﷺ said, "No servant [of Allah] in the heavens and the earth can be a believer unless he has arrived [at true belief in God], and he cannot arrive [at true belief in God] unless he is a Muslim, and he cannot be a Muslim unless people are safe from his tongue and hands, and he cannot be a Muslim unless he is knowledgeable, and he cannot be knowledgeable unless he acts upon what he knows, and he cannot act upon what he knows unless he is an ascetic, and he cannot be an ascetic unless he is God-conscious, and he cannot be God-conscious unless he is humble, and he cannot be humble unless he knows himself, and he cannot know himself unless he is intelligent and cautious in speech."

[8]

Yaḥyā ibn Muʿādh al-Rāzī said:

O you who entreats his Lord with all types of speech!
And who asks of Him residence in the Land of Peace
Who ceaselessly delays repentance year after year
I do not see you being just to your soul amongst all people
Had you but filled your day with fasting, O heedless one!
And stayed awake all night in prayer
And diminished your water and food
You would have been fit to attain the honour of elevated rank
And given the ability to perform great feats by the Lord of creation
And secured the greatest pleasure of the Possessor of Majesty and Generosity

[9]

A sage said, "Ten characteristics are hated by Allah from ten [types of] people - miserliness from the rich, arrogance from the poor, greed from scholars, lack of shame from women, love of the *dunyā* from the elderly, laziness from the youth, oppression from rulers, cowardice from warriors, self-infatuation from ascetics, and ostentation from worshippers."

[10]

The Messenger of Allah ﷺ said, "Well-being is in ten forms, five in this world and five in the next. As for those in this world, they are - knowledge, worship, *ḥalāl* income, patience in difficult times, and gratitude for blessings; as for the ones in the next world they are - the coming of the Angel of Death to the believer with mercy and gentleness; Munkar and Nakīr not frightening him in the grave; being safe on the day of the greatest terror (the Day of Judgement); the wiping away of his sins and the acceptance of his good actions; and he will pass by the *sirāṭ* [bridge over the Hellfire to be crossed by everyone on the Day of Judgement] like a flash of lightning, and will enter Paradise in peace."

[11]

Abūl Faḍl said, "Allah the Exalted has named the Qur'an with ten names - *al-Qur'an, al-Furqān* [the Criterion], *al-Kitāb* [the Book], *al-Tanzīl* [Sent Down], *al-Hudā* [the Guidance], *al-Nūr* [the Light], *al-Raḥma* [the Mercy], *al-Shifā'* [the Cure], *al-Rūḥ* [the Spirit], and *al-Dhikr* [the Remembrance]. As for its naming *al-Qur'an, al-Furqān, al-Kitāb, al-Tanzīl* it is known, as for [its naming] *al-Hudā, al-Nūr, al-Raḥma* and *al-Shifā'*, Allah the Exalted says, 'O people! A reminder has come from your Lord and a Cure for that which is in the hearts, and Guidance and Mercy for the believers.' 'And from Allah has come to you Light and a manifest Book.' As for *al-Rūḥ*, He says, 'And thus have We revealed to you a Spirit from Our command.' And as for *al-Dhikr*, He says, 'And We have revealed to you the Remembrance to make clear to people.'"

[12]

Luqmān said to his son, "Wisdom is in doing ten things - enlivening the dead heart, sitting with the needy, staying away from the gathering of kings, honouring the humble, freeing the slave, being hospitable to the stranger, enriching the poor, and venerating the people of honour. These things are better than wealth, are a protection from fear, a weapon in war, a merchandise at the time of commerce, an intercessor when afflicted with terror, an indication that conviction has entered the heart, and a covering when no clothes can cover one [on the Day of Judgement]."

[13]

A sage said, "It is incumbent upon the intelligent person when he repents to do ten things - seek forgiveness with the tongue; regret with the heart; abandon the sin with the body; resolve never to return to it (the act of disobedience); love the Hereafter; hate the *dunyā*; reduce speech; reduce food and drink so that he can devote himself to knowledge and worship; and reduce his sleep. Allah the Exalted says, 'Little did they sleep at night, and in the early hours of dawn they did seek forgiveness.'"

[14]

Anas ibn Mālik said, "Everyday the earth calls out with ten things, saying, 'O son of Adam! You strive on my surface and your destination is my stomach; you disobey [Allah] on my surface and you will be punished for it in my stomach; you laugh on my surface and you will cry in my stomach; you are happy on my surface and you will be sad in my stomach; you gather wealth on my surface and you will regret gathering it in my stomach; you eat *ḥarām* on my surface and worms will eat you in my stomach; you are arrogant on my surface and you will be humiliated in my stomach; you walk insolently on my surface and you will fall miserably into my stomach; you walk in the light on my surface and you will be in the darkness in my stomach; and you walk with crowds and large gatherings on my surface and you will be lonely in my stomach.'"

[15]

The Messenger of Allah ﷺ said, "The one who laughs a lot will be afflicted with ten things - his heart will die, he will lack shame and honour, Satan will laugh at him, [Allah] the Merciful will be angry with him, he will be held to account on the Day of Judgement, the Prophet ﷺ will turn away from him on the Day of Judgement, the angels will curse him, the people of the heavens and earth will detest him, he will forget everything, and he will be exposed on the Day of Judgement."

[16]

Al-Ḥasan al-Baṣrī said, "One day I was walking with a young pious man in the narrow streets of Baṣra and its markets until we reached a physician sitting on a chair and around him were many men, women, and children who had bottles of water in their hands. Each one of them was seeking a cure for his illness. The young man moved closer to the physician and asked him, 'O physician! Do you have a medicine that cleans away sins and cures the [spiritual] diseases of the heart?' He replied, 'Yes!' The young man said, 'Give it to me!' The physician said, 'Take ten things from me - take the roots of the tree of poverty with the roots of the tree of humility, and pour in it the milk of repentance, then place it in the mortar of acceptance [of whatever is predestined for one], crush it with the pestle of contentment, then place it in the pot of piety, pour over it the water of shame, then boil it with the fire of love, then place it in the cup of gratitude and cool it down with the fan of hope, then drink it with the spoon of praise. If you do all of this then it will cure you of every illness and trial in this world and in the Hereafter.'"

[17]

It is said that a king gathered five scholars and sages and ordered each one to give a word of wisdom. Each one spoke and gave two pieces of wisdom and thus they became ten. The first one said, "Fearing the Creator is security and feeling safe [from His wrath] is disbelief; and feeling safe from another creature is freedom and fearing him is slavery." The second said, "Hoping from Allah is richness that no poverty can harm, and losing hope in Him is poverty that no wealth can alleviate." The third said, "Poverty in worldly possessions does not harm the one rich at heart (i.e. contented), and richness in worldly possessions does not benefit the one poor at heart (i.e. greedy)." The fourth said, "Generosity does not increase the richness of the heart except in richness, and poverty at heart (greed) does not increase with richness in material possessions except in poverty." The fifth said, "Taking a little from goodness is better than leaving a lot from evil, and leaving all acts of evil is better than committing a few acts of goodness."

[18]
The Prophet ﷺ said, "There are ten types of people whose prayer Allah will not accept - the one who prays on his own without any recitation of the Qur'an; the one who does not pay the *zakāt*; the one who leads people in prayer while they detest him; the escaped slave; the alcoholic; the wife who goes to sleep at night while her husband is angry with her; the free woman who prays without a headscarf; the one who deals in interest; the oppressive leader; and the man whose prayer does not prevent him from committing acts of indecency and evil, and does not increase him except in distance from Allah the Exalted."

[19]
The Prophet ﷺ said, "Ten things are incumbent upon the one who enters the mosque - removing one's shoes; entering with the right foot; saying when entering, 'In the name of Allah and peace be upon the Messenger of Allah and the angels of Allah. O Allah open for us the doors of Your mercy, verily You are the Grantor'; greeting with salām the people of the mosque, or saying if nobody is in the mosque 'Peace be upon us and the righteous servants of Allah'; saying 'I testify that there is no Lord but Allah and that Muḥammad is the Messenger of Allah; not passing in front of those who are praying;

not engaging in worldly actions or worldly talk; not leaving without praying two *rakʿahs*; not entering [the mosque] without ablution; and saying when standing up [to leave] 'Glory and praise be to You O Allah! I testify that there is no Lord except You, I seek Your forgiveness and repent to You.'"

[20]

Abū Hurayra رضي الله عنه narrated that the Prophet ﷺ said, "Prayer is the pillar of the Religion and in it are ten benefits - beauty for the face, light for the heart, rest for the body, and escaping the loneliness of the grave. It makes mercy descend, is the key to Paradise, is heavy on the Scales [of good deeds], [gains] the pleasure of the Lord, is the price for Paradise, and the barrier against the Fire. The one who establishes it has established the Religion, and the one who leaves it has destroyed the Religion."

[21]

ʿĀ'isha رضي الله عنها narrated that the Prophet ﷺ said, "When Allah wants to allow the people of Paradise to enter Paradise, He sends them an angel with a gift and clothes from Paradise. When they're about to enter Paradise, the angel says to them, 'Wait, I have a gift with me from the Lord of the Worlds.' They will say, 'What is that gift?' The angel will say, 'It is ten seals - on the first one is written 'Peace be unto you! You were good, so enter [the Garden of delight], to dwell therein'; on the second [seal] it is written, 'Your sadness and anxieties have been removed;' written on the third is, 'And this is the garden which you are given as an inheritance on account of what you did'; written on the fourth is, 'We have given you ornaments and beautiful clothes to wear'; written on the fifth is, 'We shall wed them with *Ḥouris* with wide, lovely eyes,' and 'I have rewarded them this day because they were patient, that they are the triumphant'; written on the sixth is, 'This is your reward today for the acts of obedience you were engaged in'; on the seventh is, 'You have been returned to your youth and you will never become aged'; on the eighth is, 'You are in perpetual security and need never be frightened;' on the ninth is, 'You will be in the company of the Prophets, truthful ones, martyrs, and righteous ones'; written on the tenth is, 'You will reside beside the All-Merciful who Possesses the Great Throne.' The angels will then say, 'Enter it in peace and security.' They will thus enter Paradise and say, 'Praise is due to Allah the One who removed our anxieties, surely our Lord is Most Forgiving and Grateful.' 'Praise is due to Allah the One who was true to His Promise and gave us the inheritance of this earth... thus is the reward of those who work.'

And when Allah wishes to throw the People of Hell into the Fire, He sends them an angel who has ten seals. On the first one is written, 'Enter it, never will you die, be brought to life, or ever brought out of it'; on the second is written, 'Linger in punishment, never will there be any repose for you'; on the third is written, 'They have despaired of My mercy'; on the fourth is written, 'Enter it, into perpetual distress, anxiety, and sorrow'; on the fifth is written, 'Your clothes will be fire, your food will be from an extremely bitter and thorny tree that grows at the bottom of the Hellfire (*zaqqūm*), your drink will be boiling fluids, and your bed and covering will be the Fire'; on the sixth is written, 'This is your recompense today for disobeying Me;' on the seventh is written, 'My anger will be with you in the Fire forever;' on the eighth is written, 'You are cursed for the major sins you intentionally committed, for which you never repented nor had any regret'; on the ninth is written, 'Your eternal friends in the Fire will be the devils'; and on the tenth is written, 'You followed [the path of] Satan, desired the *dunyā* and neglected the Hereafter, thus this is your recompense.'"

[22]

A sage once said, "I sought ten things in ten places and found them in ten others - I sought elevation in arrogance but found it in humility; I sought worship in ritual prayer but found it in God-consciousness; I sought repose in greed but found it in asceticism; I sought illumination of the heart in the daytime public ritual prayers but found it in the secret late night prayers; I sought the light of the Day of Judgement in giving and generosity but found it in thirst and fasting; I sought permission to pass the *sirāṭ* in sacrificing animals [to feed the poor] but found it in giving charity (*ṣadaqa*); I sought protection from the Hellfire in permissible actions but found it in leaving desires; I sought the love of Allah the Exalted in the *dunyā* but found it in His remembrance (*dhikr*); I sought well-being in gatherings but found it in solitude; and I sought illumination of the heart in lectures and reading the Qur'an but found it in contemplation and crying."

[23]
Ibn ʿAbbās ⬥ said, "Ten things are from the *sunnah*, five related to the head and five to the body - as for the head they are: using *siwāk*, rinsing the mouth, rinsing the nose, shortening the moustache, and shaving the head. As for the body they are: removing armpit hair, clipping the nails, shaving pubic hair, circumcision, and cleansing [after relieving oneself]."

[24]
Ibn ʿAbbās ⬥ said, "The one who sends one salutation unto the Prophet ﷺ Allah will send ten salutations unto him, and the one who insults the Prophet once Allah will insult him ten times; do you not see the saying Allah the Exalted regarding al-Walīd ibn al-Mughīra, may the curse of Allah be upon him, when he insulted the Prophet ﷺ once and Allah insulted him ten times and said, 'Heed not the type of despicable men - ready with oaths, a slanderer, going about with calumnies, hinderer of the good, transgressor, malefactor, ignoble, besides all that, base-born; because he possesses wealth and (numerous) sons. That, when Our revelations are recited unto him, he says: Mere fables of the men of old.' [The last part] means that he rejected the Qur'an.

[25]
Ibrāhīm ibn Adham was asked about the saying of Allah the Exalted, 'And Your Lord said, Supplicate to me and I will answer your suppli-

cation.' "We supplicate but our prayers are not answered!" He said, "Your hearts have become dead due to ten things - you have known Allah but have not fulfilled His right; you have read the Book of Allah but did not abide by it; you proclaimed enmity of Satan but made him your guardian and protector; you claimed love of the Messenger but you left his path and his Tradition (*sunnah*); you claimed love of Paradise but you did not work for it; you claimed fear of the Hellfire but did not renounce committing sins; you claimed that you believed that death was a reality but you did not ready yourselves for it; you busied yourselves with the faults of others and neglected your own faults; you eat from the sustenance that Allah provides for you but do not show gratitude; and you bury your dead ones but do not take heed from it."

[26]

The Prophet ﷺ said, "Any servant [of Allah], whether male or female, who supplicates with this *duʿā'* - which is composed of ten phrases on the night of ʿArafa one thousand times - will not ask a thing from Allah except that He will give it to him providing he does not supplicate for the severance of ties of kinship or for an act of disobedience. The first is - glory be to the One whose Throne is in heaven; glory be to the One whose dominion and power is on earth; glory be to the One whose path is on land; glory be to the One whose Spirit is in the air; glory be to the One whose authority is in the Fire; glory be to the One whose knowledge is in the wombs; glory be to the One whose decree is in the graves; glory be to the One who raised the skies without any pillars; glory be to the One who extended the earth; glory be to the One in Whom there is no refuge or salvation except in Him."

[27]

Ibn ʿAbbās ؓ narrated that one day the Messenger of Allah ﷺ said to Satan, may the curse of Allah be upon him, "How many [types of] people are beloved to you from my *ummah*?" He said, "Ten - the oppressive ruler; the arrogant; the rich who neither care how they obtain their wealth nor how they spend it; the scholars who find excuses for the oppression of a ruler; the fraudulent trader; the one who monopolises [a product]; the fornicator; the one who deals in interest; the miser who does not care how he accumulates his wealth; and the alcoholic." The Prophet then asked, "How many [types of] people are your enemies from my *ummah*?" He said, "Twenty types [of people] - the first one is you O Muhammad, I truly hate you! [Then] the scholar who acts upon his knowledge; the one who memorises the Qur'an and fulfils its commandments; the muezzin for the five daily prayers who calls the *adhān* only for the sake of Allah; the one who loves the poor, needy, and orphans; the one who has a merciful heart; the one who humbles himself in front of the truth; the young man who grows up in the obedience of Allah the Exalted; the one who eats only *ḥalāl*; the two young men who love each other for the sake of Allah; the one who is always zealous in performing his prayers in congregation; the one who offers prayers at night while people are asleep; the one who holds his nafs back from committing the *ḥarām*; the one who advises [in another narration, supplicates for] his brothers without having any ulterior motive in his heart; the one who is always in a state of ablution; the one who is generous; the one with good manners and character; the one who believes in what His Lord has guaranteed for him; the one who does good to widows; and the one who readies himself for death."

[28]

Wahb ibn Munabbih said, "It is written in the Torah, 'He who prepares provisions [for the Hereafter] in this world will be safe from Allah's punishment on the Day of Judgement; he who leaves hatred will be praised on the Day of Judgement in front of the whole of creation; he who abandons love of leadership will be honoured on the Day of Judgement in front of the Omnipotent King; he who abandons the excesses of the *dunyā* will be blissful amongst the righteous ones [on the Day of Judgement]; he who abandons quarrelling in this world will be amongst the winners on the Day of Judgement; he who abandons miserliness in this world will be mentioned in front of the whole of creation on the Day of Judgement; he who abandons repose in this world will be happy on the Day of Judgement; he who abandons the prohibited in this world will be in the company of the Prophets on the Day of Judgement; he who abandons looking at that which has been prohibited in this world, Allah will delight his eyes on the Day of Judgement in Paradise; he who abandons wealth and chooses poverty in this world, Allah will raise him on the Day of Judgement amongst the beloved and the Prophets of Allah; he who assists others in fulfilling their needs, Allah will make him free from all needs in this world and in the next. He who wishes to have good company instead of solitude in his grave should wake up in the darkness of the night and pray; he who wishes to be in the shade of the Throne of the Merciful should become an ascetic; he who wishes his bringing to account to be easy should advise himself and his brothers; he who wishes the angels to be his visitors should become God-conscious; he who wishes to live in the delight of Paradise should remember Allah during the night and day; he who wishes to enter Paradise without any bringing to account should repent to Allah with a sincere repentance; he who wishes to be rich should become contented with what Allah the Exalted has allotted for him; he who wishes to be a man of understanding in the sight of Allah should have fear of Allah; he who wishes to be wise should seek knowledge; he who wishes to be safe from people should not mention anyone except with good and take a lesson from his own self and ponder over why and from what he was created; he who wants dignity and honour in both the *dunyā* and in the Hereafter should give preference to the Hereafter over the *dunyā*; he who wishes for *al-firdaws* (the highest rank in Paradise) and infinite happiness should not waste his life in the vices of the *dunyā*; he who wishes for Paradise in this world and the next should adopt the path of generosity, because the one who is generous is close to Paradise and far from Hell; he who wishes his heart to be enlightened with the complete light should adopt the path of contemplation and of taking lessons [from life and creation]; he who wishes to have a body that patiently endures [hardships], a tongue that is in constant remembrance [of Allah], and a heart which is fearful [of Him] should adopt the path of seeking forgiveness for the believers - male and female, and for the Muslims - male and female."